PRAYERS IN LARGE PRINT

Rita F. Snowden is widely known in many countries and is the author of more than sixty books for adults and children. After six years at business she trained as a deaconess of the New Zealand Methodist Church, serving in turn two pioneer country areas before moving to the largest city for several years of social work during an economic depression.

Miss Snowden has served the world Church, beyond her own denomination, with regular broadcasting commitments. She has written and spoken in Britain, Canada, the United States, in Australia, and in Tonga at the invitation of Queen Salote. She has represented her church at the World Methodist Conference in Oxford; later being elected the first woman Vice-President of the New Zealand Methodist Church, and President of its Deaconess Association. She is an Honorary Vice-President of the New Zealand Women Writers' Society, a Fellow of the International Institute of Art and Letters, and a member of P.E.N.

Miss Snowden has been honoured by the award of the Order of the British Empire, and by the citation of "The Upper Room" in America.

Her most recent books are *Prayers for Busy People*, *Christianity Close to Life*, *Bedtime Stories and Prayers* (for children), *I Believe Here and Now*, *Discoveries That Delight*, *Further Good News*, *Continually Aware* and *Good Company*.

GW00598380

PRAYERS
IN LARGE PRINT

Rita F. Snowden

Collins
FOUNT PAPERBACKS

First published in Great Britain in 1985
by Fount Paperbacks, London

Copyright © Rita F. Snowden 1985

Made and printed in Great Britain by
William Collins Sons & Co. Ltd, Glasgow

DEDICATED TO
my friends Dr Maxi Dunnam
and his dear wife Jerry

CONTENTS

PREFACE

Once, the smallness of print hardly mattered to me as I opened a book.

But it does now – as it does to many of my friends – and may well do so increasingly.

A wide welcome, I believe, awaits a slender book with a title like this, when it can easily be seen to live up to its title. And even more so, since it comes so close to life.

When the first Christian disciples made their request: "Lord, teach us to pray" (Luke 11:1), they were close to life, and so was He. They had seen Him at prayer. Whether He prayed audibly, and they heard Him, I do not know. Certainly they were aware of the importance of prayer to Him. Again and again, they saw Him seek out a quiet place. They saw then His features caught in rapt devotion. So they framed their petition.

Of course, they also saw Him perform miracles, and never forgot them – but they never asked Him to teach them that secret. Nor did they ask Him to teach them the secret of His unforgettable preaching. But prayer was different, it was at the heart of everything – not for getting things but for sharing communion with God.

I remembered this, of course, when I set out to write, for my own soul's strengthening, the first prayer in this book – and each time I added another. Until the book has grown to the size it is, every part of it close to life, and in this chosen large print. Interwoven are the five elements of prayer: adoration, thanksgiving, confession, petition and intercession.

Remembering these things you might try to write your own book; or you might choose this one. I mean to use it myself for a time, as a stimulus to further prayer – and of course, you are welcome to join me.

R.F.S.

PART ONE

Prayers with Bible Readings for Thirty-One Days

FIRST DAY

In the morning

God, our Father, in this place so familiar, and at my customary hour, I bring Thee my praise. Enable me to clothe my deepest thoughts in humble, honest words.

I rejoice that I am not alone in this desire to pray – many whom I know hush their hearts before Thee as a new day comes – offering as their first gifts Love, and Obedience.

From the recorded words of Jesus Christ, our Saviour and Lord, I have learned, with countless others, that Thou art a Father full of Love and utterly to be trusted.

All down the turbulent centuries since He first taught His disciples to pray – using the cherished term "Our Father", it has been constantly on the lips of those who seek Him in prayer. Save me from ever using it thoughtlessly or casually.

It is wonderful to waken to so many interests; to find myself entrusted with the power of choice. Help me to use this new day well, and bring me safely to my resting-bed when night falls.

Bless this day, I pray, all those dear to me, who support me with companionship. Save us from unkind words, and from unkind silences. Let our dealings show the graciousness of Christ.

We each have many thoughts as this day opens – but none come as a surprise to Thee, Who knowest all and desirest only the best for each of us. Give me a pliable spirit this day, let me show eagerness, and yet the gentle gift of serenity. Give me courage to face any new truth that presents itself.

Let me put the needs of others before those of myself. And, O God, have mercy on all for whom this is a bitter dawn, all who have spent a sleepless night through anxiety.

AMEN

In the evening

Gracious Father, I am glad that I do not need to pretend during prayer. I am tired now, and my words do not come easily. I have not kept all my secret promises of the morning – Father, forgive me. And as I come to my rest, let me lie down thankfully, peacefully, but not forgetting those who must work whilst I sleep – doctors and nurses, and everyone with responsibilities in places of healing or of character-correction in institutions. Grant skill to all in charge, as well as good judgement, unvarying patience and Love. In the Name of Christ.

AMEN

Daily Reading

It is good to give thanks to the Lord,
    to sing praises to thy name, O Most High;
to declare thy steadfast love in the morning,
    and thy faithfulness by night,
to the music of the lute and the harp,
    to the melody of the lyre.
For thou, O Lord, hast made me glad by thy work;
    at the works of thy hands I sing for joy.

Psalm 92:1–4

SECOND DAY

In the morning

This morning, O Lord, I bring to Thee my thanks for the sweet refreshment of sleep.

Show me how best to use my renewed energies. Let me move amongst folk with a smiling face, and a serene spirit.

There are questions which plague my mind from time to time; but none is too much for Thy glorious powers.

Give me patience when, like others, I want all things righted in a moment. In our most sensible judgements, we know that often this cannot be.

History speaks to us through the slow centuries, in order that we might trust; as good men and women have interpreted situations before us.

Let our homes know peace, and the preservation of things worthwhile. Let those who cross over our doorsteps find an oasis of beautiful contentment.

Keep us mindful of the price others have paid to prepare for us at birth, as a welcome into this world.

When the time comes, let us pass on our way with a rich sense of gratitude. So may the generations bring glory to Thy Name.

We beseech Thee, answer this prayer, forgiving all that is of human fault within it; for Christ's sake.   AMEN

In the evening

This has been a lovely day, O God. The things of Nature around have continually reminded us of Thy creative powers.

The sky above us, the earth beneath us; the flowering
gardens and parks that men and women, working with
Thee, have made,
all the colours and fragrances about us, are such a
delight! – the shapes of mountains and fields, the
rivers making their way to the sea.
Let us not be unmindful of the tiny things – wild flowers
beside our paths across the fields.
Show us how best to pass on this joy to little ones
growing up beside us, who will inherit Nature's riches.
Our Master Jesus found so much among growing things
to remind Him of Thy care. Support us all with the
same assurance, we pray.
And let us together take care of all living creatures,
especially pets during holiday times. Let us keep
loving concern alive. AMEN

Daily Reading

In many and various ways God spoke of old to our
fathers by the prophets; but in these last days he has
spoken to us by a Son, whom he appointed the heir of
all things, through whom also he created the world. He
reflects the glory of God and bears the very stamp of his
nature, upholding the universe by his word of power.
When he had made purification for sins, he sat down at
the right hand of the Majesty on high, having become
as much superior to angels as the name he has obtained
is more excellent than theirs.

Hebrews 1:1–4

THIRD DAY

In the morning

Creator God, I rejoice in the dawn that issues in this day; and all that it promises.

I praise Thee for the miracle of the seasons, with fruit and flowers; I lift mine eyes to green hills.

Fields spread out with simple delights; and beyond is the ever-pulsing life of the sea.

Plains and prairies afar support life in other parts; deserts and deep canyons hold their own secrets. (But nuclear energies spell terror.)

We have to confess that much of our good earth has fallen to a struggle between good and evil. The sharing of life's riches has passed many by.

Many of us long for the day when such good things will be commonly enjoyed, and money values will count less in the earth than today.

Show us how to seek Peace and pursue it, we pray Thee; of whatever colour or clime, we are all Thy children.

We rejoice when cures for bodily ills are ours, thanks to unknown discoverers and specialists in other lands.

We give thanks for benefits through books, and music, art and Scripture; these go on enriching us.

Our Father, we can never be thankful enough for the privilege of belonging to Thy great earth-family.

AMEN

In the evening

Gracious Father, I bless Thee for day's end, when the weary can relax – our Master and Lord many a time knew such a good gift.

17

Sometimes He sought peace in the hills and time to pray,
with the refreshment that brought;
at other times He moved unnoticed from crowded places
to the quiet beach beloved of fishermen friends.
On the desperate evening of a last supper shared with
all Twelve, He found His way to Gethsemane's
garden.
And those of us the world calls "disciples" today can
think of no richer night of their association.
But we treasure a later promise He made after His
Resurrection: "Lo, I am with you alway, even unto
the end of the world."
This assurance is still ours, we know – not by sight, but
by Faith! And we give Thee life-long thanks! AMEN

Daily Reading
He made the disciples get into the boat and go before
him to the other side . . . And after he had dismissed the
crowds, he went up on the mountain by himself to pray.
When evening came, he was there alone, but the boat
by this time was many furlongs distant from the land,
beaten by the waves; for the wind was against them. And
in the fourth watch of the night he came to them,
walking on the sea . . . And they cried out for fear. But
immediately he spoke to them, saying, "Take heart, it
is I; have no fear."

Matthew 14:22–27

FOURTH DAY

In the morning

O God, it is wonderful to waken again – to take my place in this great world of Thy creation.

I marvel at its vastness and variety; at its arching sky, its floating clouds, and constellations on high.

I pray for all who rise to serve their fellows this day – for bus drivers, and postmen especially, so seldom in my prayers.

Keep them fit and safe as they serve, rejecting all slovenliness. And sustain with perseverance all who seek work, and find none.

Let those of us blessed with work of our own choosing, use the hours of this day to Thine honour and glory, I pray.

I remember thankfully the good work given in the humble workshop of the Carpenter, long ago. Let me work as well, today.

Deliver me, O God, from the tyranny of trifles, and let me serve a wide horizon, affecting my fellow men and women.

Strengthen all those whose heavy tasks make demands beyond their diminishing powers of body and mind,

all soon coming to retirement as just reward of their labours. Let their enlarged leisure be a fulfilling experience.

Save them from all sense of lostness, and lack of community spirit. And teach their hands new skills never before embraced.   AMEN

In the evening

Eternal Father, as this day comes to its close, I bow my head to confess known imperfections. I have been too hurried at times.

Forgive me that I have found it easier to think of my own concerns than those of others.

If any looking to me for help have not found it, I ask Thy forgiveness, in the Name of Christ, my Lord.

And as I turn to the comfort of my bed, I pray for any known to me who cannot relax; who bear a burden beyond human strength.

Suffer me not to enter into my sleep with any unhelpful pride, I pray,

but embracing Thy forgiveness, let me prepare my mind and spirit to start again eagerly, when a new day comes.

Bless this night all who minister to the unsure; to all who know loneliness, or find themselves misunderstood.

Be, as ever, close to all beneath this friendly roof. In Thy mercy, heal any who know hurts of any kind.   AMEN

Daily Reading

Jesus said:

"Beware of practising your piety before men in order to be seen by them; for then you will have no reward from your Father who is in heaven. Thus, when you give alms, sound no trumpet before you, as the hypocrites do in the synagogues and in the streets, that they may be praised by men. Truly, I say to you, they have received their reward. But when you give alms, do not let your left hand know what your right hand is doing, so that your alms may be in secret; and your Father who sees in secret will reward you. And when you pray, you must not be like the hypocrites; for they love to stand and pray in the synagogues and at the street corners, that they may be seen of men. Truly, I say to you, they have received their reward."

Matthew 6:1–5

FIFTH DAY

O God, let the door of this home – and of my heart –
this day be wide enough to receive all Thy gifts with
gratitude;

and narrow enough to shut out all foolish pride, self-
sufficiency and envy.

Bring us ever nearer to true life, to know dignity in our
days; and loving service, laughter, and joy.

Bless all with creative skills who support us – gardeners,
painters, potters, weavers, and authors of loved
books.

And bless all who enrich our community – architects,
sculptors, poets, and dramatists;

those who sing, and present the music we love; and those
who continually enhance our life through
conversation.

Gird up the courage of all faced with hard tasks, and
lighten their lot as they travel along.

The mood of the Jericho Road runs through all our lives;
let us learn the secret of the Good Samaritan.

Let practical compassion have a place in all our
relationships, in the spirit of Jesus Christ, our Master,

that this world of men and women might be a better
place for all set here to live.   AMEN

In the evening

O God, as I look back over the claims of this day, I
remember Whose I am, and Whom I serve.

Forgive me, if I have in any way disappointed Thee, I

pray. Let me rise refreshed when the new day comes, and eagerly.

I need constantly a true sense of perspective, and unwearying love. Let me do my ordinary work honestly and humbly, as in Thy presence.

So may the lasting values of Christ be served, and Thy Kingdom come. I bless Thee for all – parents and preachers and friends – who have brought me into Thy presence with confidence.

Deeply and widely known today is our desperate need of Peace; let us each do what little we can to make this possible,

that Thy Name may be glorified, now and ever.　　AMEN

Daily Reading

He came to his own home, and his own people received him not. But to all who received him, who believed in his name, he gave power to become children of God; who were born, not of blood nor of the will of the flesh nor of the will of man, but of God.

And the Word became flesh and dwelt among us, full of grace and truth; we have beheld his glory, glory as of the only Son from the Father. (John bore witness to him, and cried, "This was he of whom I said, 'He who comes after me ranks before me'.") And from his fullness have we all received, grace upon grace, for the law was given through Moses; grace and truth came through Jesus Christ.

John 1:11–17

SIXTH DAY

In the morning

Gracious God, I hush my heart in this stillness, here and now; many interests claim my attention as the day opens out.

Be my Strength and Guide in this beautiful world, as I mingle with others, sharing my gift of human sensibility.

Keep me closely aware of Thy presence; from limiting selfishness and harshness, deliver me; let me draw near to people with gentleness.

Guide me moment by moment in my work, that this may be a good day; give me patience with others, intent on certain mean undertakings;

let me not be coerced by skilled advertisers to buy for myself what in this world of need, I ought not to have.

Make me a faithful steward of my earnings and spendings. Save me from being over-serious; let me add some song, some laughter to the day.

For relaxation at day's end, guide me in my choice of books; give me, when friends are free, the delight of their company.

Let warm memories of experiences shared refresh us, and add to our thanksgiving as we go on our way.

Be with the shy, and the uncertain who undertake new employment; let them find encouragement as the day proceeds.

As time goes by, enable them to establish helpful friendships, and together do good work. So let them serve Thy Kingdom.   AMEN

In the evening

O God, Thou knowest the tangled thoughts that tumble in my tired mind at times. This has been such a full day.

Again and again, when Jesus the Master was on earth, He knew a like experience. On one occasion He fell asleep in the end of Peter's boat.

One night, He had to show compassion on some close friends accompanying Him into Gethsemane to pray, since they fell asleep.

Now, as the noises and demands of this day grind to a close, I would remember before Thee the many who work while I sleep.

I thank Thee for their helpfulness; as I thank Thee, night by night, for those who provide me with clean linen, hot water and bodily comfort.

Hold in Thy safe keeping any who know fear; any who lie down with bruised spirits, with bewildered minds, with offences unforgiven.

Let them reach out to know Thy forgiveness and glorious compassion. In the Name of our Saviour Christ, I pray. AMEN

Daily Reading

Jesus said:

"Every one then who hears these words of mine and does them will be like a wise man who built his house upon the rock; and the rain fell, and the floods came, and the winds blew and beat upon that house, but it did not fall, because it had been founded on the rock. And every one who hears these words of mine and does not

25

do them will be like a foolish man who built his house upon the sand; and the rain fell, and the floods came, and the winds blew and beat against that house, and it fell; and great was the fall of it."

Matthew 7:24–27

SEVENTH DAY

In the morning

Gracious God, Creator of all good, I am comforted to think that the kindly light that greets my eyes on waking just now is Thine;

that the breath in my lungs, and the strength in my limbs are Thine. We men and women of earth are not sufficient unto ourselves.

Let me take good care of these gracious gifts today, I pray Thee, and do nothing deliberately to injure the lot of others.

I think especially of the many who unhappily find themselves in hospital; or in court; or in prison.

Deliver those who tend them from any sense of self-importance, and strengthen their reliability when routine tasks bring weariness.

Guide all who work with steady minds and imaginations; and all those who work with their hands at others' bidding.

Enable all who work alone to do so as in Thy sight, and as faithfully as if all the world saw.

Hold in Thy keeping young couples setting up new homes. Bless any I know now entering on the joys of parenthood.

Strengthen and support the tired and frail, I pray, and give them a fund of happy memories to ponder, and kindly thoughts.   AMEN

In the evening

O God, as the sun sinks in the west and night comes, I join many of Thy children who seek Thee in prayer.

It is wonderful that we are never, under any circumstances, wholly alone – always Thou art near.

With joy I have seen new sights today; have met new people; and had new thoughts visit my mind.

For all such gifts, I bring Thee my thanks at day's end. Enable me, in turn, to enrich others whom I meet.

I give Thee thanks for warm and dependable friends; for some gifted with fine minds, and some with practical skills.

Others are endowed with music and song; and yet others with the proverbial "green fingers" to garden and beautify the earth.

So are we trebly blessed with fruits, colours, and fragrances. And for all these good things we praise Thee.   AMEN

Daily Reading

Lord, thou hast been our dwelling place
    in all generations.
Before the mountains were brought forth,
    or ever thou hadst formed the earth
        and the world,
        from everlasting to everlasting thou
            art God.

Thou turnest man back to the dust, and
    sayest: "Turn back, O children of men!"

For a thousand years in thy sight are
  but as yesterday when it is past,
  or as a watch in the night.

Psalm 90:1–4

EIGHTH DAY

In the morning

Eternal God, Creator of all things beautiful and true, Thou art also Keeper and Sustainer of all things.

Save me today from any sense of insecurity, from any human stubbornness or self-importance. Let me mingle with those about me.

Save me from any religious pretence; from any unwillingness to serve. May there be no inconsistency in what I say and do.

I know that no failure in this is beyond forgiveness; that no weakness need be carried into a new day.

May all whose hearts are set on Peace among the nations, know Thy sustaining presence this day.

May those living in lands not their own, be helpful in any way that they can; and enrich lives.

Guide the youthful into true plans for the future; and let the elderly support them with kindly understanding.

We ask that together – with our various gifts of nature and training – we may draw closer.

Break down everywhere divisions of pride or possessions, any foolish claims made for colour or clime.

We are all Thy children; let the Spirit of Christ guide us this day.   AMEN

In the evening

From everlasting to everlasting, O Lord, Thou art our loving Creator and Preserver. We bless Thee for this assurance.

And now as night gathers about us like a comfortable cloak, we bring Thee our adoration and thanks, our unquestionable love.

Graciously support this night all who are sick, all who are sad; and grant strength of body, and gentleness of touch to all nearby them.

So may they be saved from despair, and from lack of co-operation. Give us all some new happiness to share in this time together.

Keep us sensitive to each other's needs, and endlessly patient; that, aware of Thy will, we might move towards wholeness.

We bless Thee for windows bringing in Thy gifts of light and air; for flowers and fruits, arts and all colourful, lovely things.

And we bless Thee for all good books, papers and songs that support our thought; and for the delight of friendly conversation.   AMEN

Daily Reading
Have this mind among yourselves, which is yours in Christ Jesus, who, though he was in the form of God, did not count equality with God a thing to be grasped, but emptied himself, taking the form of a servant, being born in the likeness of men. And being found in human form he humbled himself and became obedient unto death, even death on a cross. Therefore God has highly exalted him and bestowed on him the name which is above every name, that at the name of Jesus every knee should bow, in heaven and on earth and under the earth,

and every tongue confess that Jesus Christ is Lord, to the glory of God the Father.

Philippians 2:5–11

NINTH DAY

In the morning

At first light, O Lord, the coming of the newspaper, and the voice of the radio remind me of many human interests.

I offer my spoken petitions for all in positions of trust; for all in government, all in commerce, in travel and transport.

I seek Thy help for all whose work is in the home; and for all serving, in many ways, the stewardship of the land.

Support especially those who teach small children this day, and those whose work is to lead energetic youth.

Give knowledge and patience to all who tend animals, and let working requirements be sensible of their strength.

Bless all, young and old, who have pets – keep them ever mindful of their healthful needs of cover, food and water.

Meet the requirements of the very many fellow humans unknown to me, living in countries newly come to independence.

Guide all those who must deal with hunger, and with riotous actions; with work dissatisfaction, and poor pay.

Quicken all in leadership everywhere; give them a strong and helpful sense of justice, and respect.

We deeply, and urgently, need Peace in this world – teach us how to fashion it, to Thy glory, and the longing of so many of us.   AMEN

In the evening

As light leaves the sky, and night descends, we express our gratitude that this world is still Thy world.

Galaxies exist within bounds of Thy mighty care, seas roll, and seasons come and go. Here Nature's colours gladden us.

And we men and women, with every earth creature, get the gift of breath from Thee.

We praise Thee for the varied gifts of movement that we know, for the homes that we build, and the delights that we share.

Trees and grass, shrubs and common wild flowers continue, and as the days pass, new strains of life appear.

We marvel at Thine infinite diversity, startling us continually. Save us from ever taking such loveliness for granted.

Make us willing to share, and to exercise tender care of these good gifts, so widely found in Thy world.   AMEN

Daily Reading

Who shall separate us from the love of Christ? Shall tribulation, or distress, or persecution, or famine, or nakedness, or peril, or sword?

As it is written,

"For thy sake we are being killed all the day long;
we are regarded as sheep to be slaughtered."

No, in all these things we are more than conquerors through him who loved us. For I am sure that neither death, nor life, nor angels, nor principalities, nor things present, nor things to come, nor powers, nor height, nor depth, nor anything else in all creation, will be able to separate us from the love of God in Christ Jesus our Lord.

Romans 8:35–39

TENTH DAY

In the morning
Eternal God, it is a continual wonder that, morning by morning, I am allowed to open my eyes amidst the marvels of this great universe. From age to age, with the breaking of the day, men and women have paused to praise Thee – and in my own way, I do that now.

I praise Thee for the rising sun; and for the seasons that visit the earth, each with its flowers and fruits that are a never-ending delight. I praise Thee for living shapes and colours, all around – and never to be taken for granted.

And to match them, I thank Thee for the sharp co-operation of endowed senses to register appreciation and know Thy gifts for what they are: things ever needful, ever changing. I praise Thee for stout trees affording shelter, and their tiny twigs filigreed against the sky. For the patterns of fields and hedges, and the productiveness of tilled soil. Few of us are far from these seasonal gifts, for although we live in cities we can refresh our tired bodies and minds in walks or rides out amongst them. I bless Thee for men and women of the countryside, who by their honest purpose and hard toil serve Thine on-going Will.

Grant this day, to all who tend and all who harvest, a due sense of responsibility. Deliver us all from marketing greed that holds back what others – for their very life – have need of.

Above all, I rejoice that in the fullness of Time Thou

hast revealed Thy heart not only in these natural things but in the changeless life and spirit of Jesus Christ, our Lord.   AMEN

In the evening

Beloved Creator and Loving Keeper, I give Thee thanks for the stars steady above, the sweet airs about me, and that Thou hast entrusted to me this day the swift and gracious gifts of life herewith many good men and women, filling my mind with welcome thoughts, and have girdled my comings and goings with Love.

Now, as I surrender my powers in sleep, forgive me anything that would rise up to disturb my relationship with Thee. Let no remembrance of this day mar my peace of heart and mind, I pray Thee. And in Thy Love sustain and keep this night all those who are dear to me, for Christ's sake.   AMEN

Daily Reading

The law of the Lord is perfect,
    reviving the soul;
the testimony of the Lord is sure,
    making wise the simple;
the precepts of the Lord are right,
    rejoicing the heart;
the commandment of the Lord is pure,
    enlightening the eyes;
the fear of the Lord is clean,
    enduring for ever;

the ordinances of the Lord are true,
    and righteous altogether.
More to be desired are they than gold,
    even much fine gold.

Psalm 19:7–10

ELEVENTH DAY

In the morning

Last night, O Lord, I was so tired at nightfall. My energies are not what they used to be. But now, through sleep, I am renewed.

My first thoughts are to give thanks for ordinary things – breath in my lungs, thoughts in my mind, and bodily strength.

Thou hast given me more precious powers than the wild things know, and above all, a spirit fashioned for Thy companionship.

Bless all beloved human beings beneath this roof, and scatter any easy excuse that holds us back from giving help.

Thou hast set us each here to offer support, day by day. Thou hast endowed us with various gifts and characters.

Some of us have lively minds; others mere practical gifts; others again are fashioners and fixers of things. Some garden; some offer music.

Keep us wide awake as each new day comes – employing our training, reading and travelling in useful ways.

Save us from jealousy, as we look at others' accomplishments; let ours be ever dedicated hands, used fully.

Give us glad persistence as strength and imaginative skills diminish and infirmities multiply. We would lovingly serve Thee for ever.   AMEN

In the evening

As darkness wraps us round and stars come out, O God,
I hush my heart. Earth-noises of the busy day are
quieted – as they need to be.

I rejoice in this moment, since I must get things into
perspective if life is to be meaningful.

Thou hast set me to live in this time and in this place;
and I give Thee thanks for all who come over my
doorstep.

Let no unworthy pride have a place in my daily comings
and goings. We share each other's interests; faith and
books, fruits and flowers.

So with the passing years, rich memories have been built
up. Music and song have surrounded us. And we enter
into the gifts of Art.

The loveliness of earth's changing seasons has long
delighted us. And we go on giving Thee praise for the
freshness of little children; for the vigour of youth, the
earnestness of middle years, the quiet wisdom of
maturity, and the gentleness of old age. So does my
heart speak. AMEN

Daily Reading

The Lord is my shepherd; I shall not want.
He maketh me to lie down in green pastures:
he leadeth me beside the still waters.
He restoreth my soul:
he leadeth me in the paths
    of righteousness for his name's sake.
Yea, though I walk through the valley of the
    shadow of death,

I will fear no evil: for thou art
  with me;
thy rod and thy staff they comfort me.
Thou preparest a table before me in the presence of
  mine enemies:
thou anointest my head with oil;
  my cup runneth over.
Surely goodness and mercy shall follow me all the
  days of my life;
and I will dwell in the house
  of the Lord for ever.

Psalm 23 (*Authorized Version*)

TWELFTH DAY

In the morning

Gracious God, I rejoice in the gift of this new day. As its clean light streams in, I give Thee thanks for the good gift of sleep.

And I remember now the sleepless sick; and all the troubled and fearful, who face this day's responsibilities unrefreshed.

Nor would I forget those who have chosen to give night service to their fellows – doctors and nurses, firemen, and caretakers, policemen, airline pilots and crew; and train drivers, boring through the darkness.

And I remember that, through calm and storm, there are captains of seagoing ships, and their crews, who assume responsibility for other people's lives.

Strengthen and support those who set about new tasks – and no less, those long grown weary in their old tasks, but who still go on.

I pray especially for all in places of leadership, whose judgements affect so many lives.

I ask for essential gifts of friendliness and patience, for all who deal daily with the young, all who teach or lead.

Bless all editors, journalists and authors exercising a ministry of print, affecting community standards and widespread behaviour.

And those who invade many homes, through the media of television, transistors and regular magazines. May life be enriched by them, I pray Thee.   AMEN

In the evening

O Lord of life in its infinite variety, I praise Thee for the
interest and delight that this day's sharing has brought
to me.

I bless Thee for the energies, the gifts and graces of
many close to my life – good gardeners, preachers,
and story-tellers.

I rejoice in a special few who add music and song to my
life, and all the many who prepare and serve good
meals in hospitality.

I am enriched by many ready to share experiences; all
prepared to lend their best-loved books; or to be
generous with their cars.

Without fear, I bring to Thy loving scrutiny this night all
that I have done, and thought and learned this day.

Forgive me, when I have spoken in haste, where silence
would have better and have more lastingly served.

And I am thinking of some dear to me in special need
.... and .... and .... I am thankful that
each is known to Thee, and loved. AMEN

Daily Reading

And he came to Nazareth, where he had been brought
up; and he went to the synagogue, as his custom was, on
the sabbath day. And he stood up to read; and there was
given to him the book of the prophet Isaiah. He opened
the book and found the place where it was written,

"The Spirit of the Lord is upon me,
because he has anointed me
    to preach good news to the poor.

43

He has sent me to proclaim release to the captives
and recovering of sight to the blind,
to set at liberty those who are oppressed,
to proclaim the acceptable year of the Lord."

And he closed the book . . . And he began to say to
them, "Today this scripture has been fulfilled in your
hearing."

Luke 4:16–20

THIRTEENTH DAY

In the morning

This day, O Lord, open my eyes, quicken my understanding, and give me courage for whatever comes.

Save me from myself. My hope is in Christ risen from the dead, alive and ever present.

Before the clamant calls of the busy world break in upon me, renew my sense of Thy nearness.

And in Thy mercy, grant a like blessing to all dear to me just now.

Quicken in our hearts a desire to seek Thine aid, and banish all our fears.

Deliver us from the tyranny of things; in Thy patient Love show us what is important and inspire us to pursue it.

Give us open minds to accept new truth from Thee; save us from any hindering prejudices we have.

Give us the courage to be tolerant about others' judgements. Let us work together trustingly this day.

So may we go forward with new spirit into the adventure of living. In Christ's Name.   AMEN

In the evening

Gracious Father, I pray for all who just now come home tired and discouraged from their day's work.

Let them be assured of a loving welcome from those at home. From shops and gardens supply them with a good meal.

Let talk together of the day's doings bring interest, and

relaxation, stimulating company.

All too few of us wholly keep our bright promises –
forgive us, and lead us steadfastly on when a new day
comes.

We give Thee thanks for our good beds, and for
quietness and ease as sleep approaches.

Bless this night any dear to us, far from home; any
travelling; any lacking companionship.

Support especially the shy, the unsure, the
inexperienced; and bring them with hope to new
things.   AMEN

Daily Reading

God is our refuge and strength,
   a very present help in trouble.
Therefore we will not fear though the earth should
    change,
  though the mountains shake in the heart of the sea;
though its waters roar and foam,
  though the mountains tremble with
    its tumult. . . .
"Be still, and know that I am God.
  I am exalted among the nations,
  I am exalted in the earth!"

Psalm 46:1–3,10

FOURTEENTH DAY

In the morning

Gracious God, I waken to the certainty of a meal at each day's beginning – an adequate breakfast – and I give Thee thanks.

But there are millions – old and young – in the vast continent of Africa alone, who cannot know this essential need met.

All we who are well nourished, face this challenge: for many die of hunger.

We remember how once our Risen Lord called dispirited disciples to "breakfast" on the lake shore, having lighted a fire.

And there He was happy to provide food, cooked and ready. So we feel sure that He cares for the hunger of these desperate millions, and we pray for His blessing on all who serve Him in this needy task.

Some are missionaries, some are medical helpers, some are storemen.

Some move from the centre of many a grim situation to tell the world the truth; some are preachers who seek to inform congregations, or crowds gathered together.

Some are journalists who send the stirring message out in print; some are photographers, some artists who prepare posters.

It is important to spread the news, since immense numbers are on the edge of human existence.

In Thine infinite mercy, strengthen and help all who show compassion; let them today set about this immense task in the most practical way.   AMEN

In the evening

All manner of serious matters are in my mind this night, O God, as I come to rest.

I do not forget the hungry, the homeless, the sad.

I do not forget what I face often in reading my New Testament: "Let your love be a real thing" (Moffatt's rendering of Romans 12:9).

O God, it is not easy to be light-hearted in this kind of world, where so many stand in need – and so many pass them by.

Teach us, wherever we are, to behave as disciples of Christ, the Compassionate. We look to Thee for strength, and undiscourageable readiness to help.

Give us "the bi-focals of Faith", that we may keep in perspective both the needs of the far, and the needs of the near.

Our Father – as Jesus taught us to pray this way – it was with the whole of Thine earth-family in mind; we are not solitary disciples.

Thou hast "bound us together in the bundle of life" – so unearned ill comes to us all here; and unearned good. This spells "belonging".   AMEN

Daily Reading

As he went ashore he saw a great throng, and he had compassion on them . . . And when it grew late, his disciples came to him and said, "This is a lonely place . . . send them away, to go into the country and villages round about and buy themselves something to eat." . . . And he said to them, "How many loaves have you? Go and see." And when they had found out, they said,

48

"Five, and two fish." Then he commanded them all to sit down by companies upon the green grass . . . And taking the five loaves and the two fish he looked up to heaven, and blessed, and broke the loaves . . . and he divided the two fish among them all . . . And those who ate the loaves were five thousand men.

Mark 6:34–44

FIFTEENTH DAY

In the morning

Grant me readiness to rise with this new day, O God; and to serve Thee with all my powers.

Let no concern with failure yesterday hold me back today. Let me face what comes with a valiant heart, and just as it comes.

This great blessing that I ask for myself, I ask also for my friends. I think especially of any who suffer illness.

Bless any who find their splendid strength being drained away. Give them courage, I beseech Thee, and what it takes to persevere.

Bless their visitors – may they think to bring on loan a number of their best books; and to share some enheartening news.

Remind all their kindly callers to stay but a short time, that the patient may be refreshed.

O God, our Father, Thou art the final source of all that comforts and strengthens. Bless all who know this, and who act helpfully.

Bless those who set flowers in rooms; and those who prepare attractive trays – let them think of something nice to offer.

And inspire a friend here and there at a distance to send an interesting letter.

So may the long hours that seem to drag, hasten by happily, and a better day come. Jesus was often with the sick, on earth, and He cares for them still.   AMEN

In the evening

As bright colour gathers in the west, one's thoughts go
   back thankfully, O God, over the experiences of this
   day. Let me gain from them.

We remember those two dispirited men who met with
   the Risen Lord on the way to Emmaus, when their
   shadows in the dust were long drawn out.

We remember His readiness to accept their hospitality.
   Let us be as ready with the timeless words: "Abide
   with us!"

Lift the burden of sorrow from any whom we know; and
   send us on our way back to them with good news.

For Christ, Risen triumphant on this earth of many
   hurts, is the only One Who can completely change a
   day of despair.

So tender is His concern! So strong and supportive His
   love! let us share our experience with any cast down.

Quicken our feet to run back to the place of sorrow, like
   those two returning eager-hearted on the way from
   Emmaus.   AMEN

Daily Reading

By the grace given to me [wrote Paul] I bid every one
among you not to think of himself more highly than he
ought to think . . . For as in one body we have many
members, and all the members do not have the same
function, so we, though many, are one body in Christ,
and individually members one of another . . . Let love
be genuine; hate what is evil, hold fast to what is good;
love one another with brotherly affection; outdo one

51

another in showing honour. Never flag in zeal, be aglow with the Spirit, serve the Lord. Rejoice in your hope, be patient in tribulation, be constant in prayer.

Romans 12:3–4,9–12

SIXTEENTH DAY

In the morning

Gracious God, in Whose hands are the glorious issues of Life and Death, I am thankful to know Thee as Father of my spirit, and grateful that from Jesus I have learned what kind of Father Thou art.

So I come to Thee in this moment of prayer, confident and hopeful. Let me discharge gladly my routine tasks today. Let me show loving patience with those about me.

I praise Thee for what the New Testament records of the carpenter's task; that Nazareth was not a work place too modest for Thy Son; that He had daily dealings with other craftsmen and customers.

I rejoice especially that He could return there, in time, to begin His public ministry; and that no one with whom He ever dealt, could complain of shoddy, unsatisfactory workmanship.

Let my work this day, however commonplace, be as satisfactory, I pray. Let its outcome also have worth and attractiveness. Let me acknowledge that the needs of others are important.

Hold in Thy special care all who are weary of the work they must do; who are irked by relationships with those with whom they share. Give them fresh patience, and quicken between them new interest.

So may the essentials – shown in Nazareth at a bench long ago – be widely spread amongst all of us who serve today. In His Name.   AMEN

In the evening

Gracious God, from time beyond earthly remembering, the night has gathered in the weary for rest – birds flying homeward on tired wings; wild creatures, and pets, seeking out known shelter, many of them turning naturally to barns and lofts. Fathers, mothers and children have closed doors behind them, drawn curtains, and gathered thankfully together.

Bless this night all who have no shelter – and all who in any way show concern for them – the homeless, the refugees, the "street kids".

And minister to all where no love is; where drugs and drink and other abuses flourish, where the ugliness of fear and hunger lurks. Guide those who in the course of their work, as night falls, must judge awkward situations, and decide what can be done for those who have come under the law's concern. Bless all who do what they can to lead others to new beginnings. In the Name of Christ I ask this.   AMEN

Daily Reading

He went away . . . and came to his own country; and his disciples followed him. And on the sabbath he began to teach in the synagogue; and many who heard him were astonished, saying, "Where did this man get all this? What is the wisdom given to him? What mighty works are wrought by his hands! Is not this the carpenter, the son of Mary, and brother of James and Joses and Judas and Simon, and are not his sisters here with us?" . . . And Jesus said to them, "A prophet is not without honour, except in his own country, and among his own kin, and in his own house."

Mark 6:1–4

SEVENTEENTH DAY

In the morning

O God, as the birds and furry creatures waken and make themselves heard, may our more meaningful praises rise to Thee.

We find joy in the natural sounds and scents about us, and in many lovely shapes and colours.

From the beginning of Time, psalmists, saints and songsters have shared these delights.

Bless all good gardeners, all artists in pigments and clays, all who erect noble buildings, or share truth in words.

Bless all parents, fashioning for the world of tomorrow strong bodies and fine personalities.

Support teachers, and sports leaders, that leisure as well as work may be offered to Thy glory.

Guide our national and international leaders, that justice might be established in the earth.

Support all set on Peace in the dealings of men and women everywhere, I pray, that wars may cease.

Guide those responsible for the affairs of our cities – mayors, councillors and all under them who are concerned for good.

Support all whose energies and homes are set upon farming lands, who can know but few neighbours, and are sometimes very lonely.   AMEN

In the evening

O Lord, I rejoice that no part of this earth-life is untouched by Thy loving care.

So many things change with the swift passage of Time.
Quieten my spirit and strengthen my faith in Thee, O
Lord.

Forbid that I should despise anyone about me. Save me
from hasty criticism or prideful superiority.

Establish in my heart the secret of the Good Samaritan;
let none lie untended where I pass along, I pray.

Grant Thy holy keeping this night to any who are
strangers or lonely hereabouts. Father of us all, our
true security is in Thee.

Keep us lastingly aware of the preciousness of life, O
Lord. And now let me surrender to Thee at bedtime
this day's service.

Without Thee, nothing is great, nothing is finally
significant. In this faith, I come to my sleep. AMEN

Daily Reading
Paul wrote:
You were called to freedom . . . only do not use your
freedom as an opportunity for the flesh, but through
love be servants of one another. For the whole law is
fulfilled in one word, "You shall love your neighbour as
yourself." . . . The fruit of the Spirit is love, joy, peace,
patience, kindness, goodness, faithfulness, gentleness,
self-control; against such there is no law. And those who
belong to Christ Jesus have crucified the flesh with its
passions and desires. If we live by the Spirit, let us also
walk by the Spirit.

Galatians 5:13–14,22–25

In the morning

Great Giver of Life, as I return to awareness I remember all who through human carelessness, awaken to hunger and thirst this day.

Excuses are useless – we need Thy forgiveness and Thy readiness in Christ to help all in illness or despair.

Thou hast endowed us with many gifts and graces – help us to share fully. Let no pride or narrowness of experience ever spoil this.

As we go about our affairs, let us not act as individuals, but as members of this earth-family which Thou hast created.

I give thanks for the rich blessings of memory, especially for every recollection of loving fellowship with others.

Let me go on sharing the fruits and flowers of my garden, and the savings of my purse, where such will serve.

Let me offer hospitality, and, like those of Emmaus, use my home to support it. There may we all know the Presence of Christ.

Let me guard my speech this day, that it may not sharpen into gossip; let my ears be willing to receive only what is true.

Bless this day all whose first thoughts are for others – social workers, deaconesses, ministers, priests, nurses, nuns and doctors.

Have mercy on all who falter in these tests that life brings, and save them from falling. For Thy Kingdom's sake. AMEN

In the evening

Lord of lasting Life, as this day reaches its close Thou knowest what new people I have met, and what new ideas have come to me.

You know when my words of cheer have helped some other along. Forgive me if I have anywhere dropped unkindly criticism.

I bless Thee for my physical well-being; for my home, and its regular meals; for letters, and expressions of loving care.

I praise Thee for my church, and all with whom I regularly worship. Bless both young and old, and all those as yet only mid-way through life.

Strengthen our ongoing witness to the Love of Christ, and let us widen as we can this redeeming experience.

Support all preachers, Christian authors, singers and musicians, missionaries, and distributors of Scripture.

So may the time soon come when no living soul anywhere shall be without knowledge of Thy Love.

AMEN

Daily Reading

By this we know love, that he laid down his life for us; and we ought to lay down our lives for the brethren. But if any one has the world's goods and sees his brother in need, yet closes his heart against him, how does God's love abide in him? Little children, let us not love in word or speech but in deed and in truth.

By this we shall know that we are of the truth, and reassure our hearts before him whenever our hearts condemn us; for God is greater than our hearts, and he knows everything.

1 John 3:16–20

NINETEENTH DAY

In the morning

As I awaken, Gracious God, on this given morning, all
  my senses tell me that every good and lovely thing
  comes from Thee.

So my first words are centred on thanksgiving. It is
  wonderful to greet the early light which was Thy first
  creative gift to this world, and still remains
  undiminished.

Every tiny green shoot, every up-reaching tree, every
  flowerbud makes its natural response.

But here and now my own response is many times more
  meaningful because Thou hast given me body, mind
  and spirit – a unique capacity to receive such a gift.

I thank Thee for it especially this morning, having in
  mind those who must move this day through sickness,
  suffering and weakness. May it speak a message of
  Hope to them.

Give to all who tend them – added to their skills and
  along with the advanced powers of medical support –
  a kindly, encouraging spirit, I pray.

I think especially this lovely morning, of what it will
  mean to certain friends .... and .... and
  ....

Receive my thanks for Thy generous gifts to all who
  have grown too frail to order their own affairs. In the
  Name of Christ, the Compassionate.   AMEN

In the evening

Our Father, we have to confess that many of us find it

61

easier to deal with things than with people. We sometimes lack sweet patience. Please forgive us.

Jesus, our Saviour and Lord, has shown us how to deal with fellow men and women, in sickness and in health. Forgive us that ever we overlook this glorious reality.

Forgive us too that ever we are over-hasty in our judgements, over-mastered often by shortness of experience.

Breathe Thy Spirit into the hearts of all those of us who must care for those who have come to the end of this earth-life.

From the dawn of Time, men and women have trusted Thee fully – and so we do that now. In Christ's Name.

AMEN

Daily Reading

Have you not known? Have you not heard?
The Lord is the everlasting God,
 the Creator of the ends of the
  earth.
He does not faint or grow weary,
 his understanding is unsearchable,
He gives power to the faint,
 and to him who has no might he increases
  strength.

Isaiah 40:28–29

TWENTIETH DAY

In the morning

I rejoice in the light of this new day, O God, for its gifts, and for every promise of things lastingly good and to be remembered.

Thou hast set within our human hands powers that are precious. Strengthen us each, as we go upon our way.

Enable us to forgive others, even as we have ourselves been forgiven, in the Name of Christ our Lord.

Bless any newly literate, as they discover for themselves the Old and New Testament Scriptures.

Enable them to know, in very truth, the Redeeming Love of Christ, our Risen Lord.

Bless all who share their knowledge and love in the translation of Christian literature; bless those in the Bible Societies, and in Christian bookshops.

Forgive all those of us whose efforts are spasmodic. Teach us the joy of sustained effort. Bless all who serve "till nightfall".

Inspire all who share the Gospel through drama, through radio, and through television.

Thou hast lighted within our human spirits a flame that will never go out. For this wonder I bless Thee.   AMEN

In the evening

O God, as night falls I give Thee thanks for the gifts of this day – for food and clothing; for fresh air; for new thoughts.

This never ceases to hold fascination for me, and I lift

my heart in praise as countless men and women before me have done.

I bless Thee for Thine ever-widening revelation in Christ, and I beseech Thee, deliver me from all casualness.

Let me never be found gazing afar, when all the time Thou hast tasks awaiting me close at hand.

May no "burning bush" declare Thy presence, and I fail to notice it. For open eyes, and shoes shed, I bless Thee on any desert's rim.

Enlarge what I know of courage, integrity, and faithfulness, O God. Let me never slump in my humble serving.

Let me rejoice in Thy Kingdom, as long as I live, and at last, in Thy mercy, receive me into Thy immediate presence. AMEN

Daily Reading

Even youths shall faint and be weary,
    and young men shall fall exhausted;
but they who wait for the Lord shall
    renew their strength,
    they shall mount up with wings like eagles,
they shall run and not be weary,
    they shall walk and not faint.

Isaiah 40:30–31

TWENTY-FIRST DAY

In the morning

Oh God, send me out into this new day with eagerness, and bring me in again at nightfall unashamed.

I give Thee my thanks for the continuing intimate joys of home; for the helpful outreach of neighbours.

I pray for social workers, mayors, ministers and teachers, and all who attempt to establish fair dealing in the community.

Let the sacredness of personality be honoured, along with the lasting worth of good deeds. Let Love be at the heart of all we do.

So may the values of Christ, our Master, flourish amongst us; so may Thy lasting Kingdom be served.

Bless every glimmering of goodness – fan it with Thy Spirit. Strengthen the leaders of our country, and let justice and peace be established.

Whatever calls for my care today, among things near or far, let me be found faithful in my response.

I praise Thee for the challenging New Testament teaching that walks up and down in my mind; and for what truth has come through earlier writings.

I praise Thee for prophets, psalmists and saints from the very dawn of Time; and for the many now, in Thy modern world.

Sometimes newspaper headlines spoil my assurance of this shining reality. Yet is my hope rooted wholly in Thy purpose. AMEN

In the evening

Eternal God, I rejoice that in every generation fine men and women have come forth to worship Thee – and not only in words.

And that, away back, beyond the first written record, homes have been established, however modest in structure.

Little children have been born, and tended lovingly, to grow up to serve others besides their own families.

I bless Thee for writers of good books; for makers of songs; and for so many beautiful things to add to daily life.

I rejoice above all that, as time moved on, Jesus came from a home in Nazareth, to set earthly things in proper perspective.

I rejoice that in His ministry He set no hard line between the sacred and the secular. In His sight all served to support life.

Let all men and women, the world over – not forgetting our own – know this secret, and for ever serve Thy holy purpose.   AMEN

Daily Reading

Moses was keeping the flock of his father-in-law, Jethro, the priest of Midian; and he led his flock to the west side of the wilderness, and came to Horeb, the mountain of God. And the angel of the Lord appeared to him in a flame of fire out of the midst of a bush; and he looked, and lo, the bush was burning, yet it was not consumed. And Moses said, "I will turn aside and see this great sight, why the bush is not burnt." When the Lord saw that he turned aside to see, God called to him out of the bush, "Moses, Moses!" And he said, "Here am I!"

Exodus 3:1–4

TWENTY-SECOND DAY

In the morning

O God, I open my eyes, and my heart turns toward Thee in praise –

> I rejoice in my setting, amidst things reassuring and familiar;
>
> I rejoice in the beauty of growing, knowing things:
>
> In birds on topmost twigs and lines;
>
> In pets. In passers-by going to their work.
>
> Most of all, I rejoice in my capacity to do things myself.

Enable me to live well this day, and enlarge the worth of my service.

I seek Thy blessing on all whom I love .... and .... and ....

Sustain this day, I pray, all those who are lonely, or frustrated.

Forgive and heal the wilful and irresponsible.

Draw near to all in institutions, and those who care for them.

Let a new sense of justice come to our community, where strife is.

> Bless especially this day, all entering into marriage.
>
> Bless those establishing new homes, and gardens.
>
> Bless those setting about new occupations with hesitancy.
>
> Bless those fully assured, and long established –
>
> Save them from becoming over-casual, or lacking in co-operation.

Let respect, and true consideration continue this
   day.
And so bring us to the close of the working day with
   satisfaction, and a humble pride in our contribution to
   life. For Christ's sake.   AMEN

In the evening

Bless, O God, as the day closes, all who have spent it
   at home, and those who have been out with many
   others at work.
Bless us, as we talk together of the interesting events of
   the day: new words and doings of little children;
   refreshing visits and undertakings.
Bless those afar, whose letters have reached us by post,
   and all who have taken pains to phone during the day.
Bless those always close, and established in love, I
   pray. They have brought much enrichment to our
   lives.
Sustain those who have known disappointment of any
   kind, this day; let them be ready to start again
   tomorrow.
Bless those who know physical difficulties as the years
   go on, and all who minister to them, with knowledge
   and gentleness.
And so bring us to our resting-beds with thanksgiving,
   to be restored to ongoing life again tomorrow.   AMEN

Daily Reading
 Though I walk in the midst of trouble,
    thou dost preserve my life;

thou dost stretch out thy hand against
    the wrath of my enemies,
  and thy right hand delivers me.
The Lord will fulfil his purpose for me;
  thy steadfast love, O Lord, endures for ever.
  Do not forsake the work of thy hands.

Psalm 138:7–8

In the morning

Gracious Father of my spirit, Whose Eternal nature I partly know, and partly do not know, I come to Thee in prayer.

Jesus my Lord, long ago, won me to this trustful experience, as He taught His first disciples to pray, "Our Father".

Forgive me, if ever I have taken this privilege of right – if ever I have forgotten that I am Thy child.

It is wonderful to waken to this new day – to feel the air about me, and know my body fit.

It is good to know human relationships at every turn; to work, and plan, and sing together during this day.

I bless Thee for little children and their simplicity; for teenagers and their energies;

for steady, dependable middle-aged men and women; for old folks, a long life of experience behind them.

Forgive me, if ever I have lowered my standards for popularity; forgive me, if ever I have refused a difficult task.

No two mornings are ever wholly alike – but Thy Redeeming Love, interpreted on the Cross, remains for ever constant.

Beyond that, I have accepted the reality of the Risen Christ triumphant, and He wins my adoration, here and for ever. AMEN

In the evening

Eternal God, so many happenings of each day delight me that I must raise my voice in praise, before I come to my sleep.

I have not always the best words in which to express what I deeply feel – but all my longings Thou dost understand.

I bless Thee for the friends Thou hast given me; for the countless lovely books I have; for the music I have listened to.

I look back with joy on the many journeys I have made; I think of trees, streams and gardens, and lastingly beautiful places.

I bless Thee for many fine ordinary people who have well and widely interpreted the joys of family life.

I rejoice that when I pause to pray, I have never any cause to pretend; Thy Love and Mercy here and now are beyond all telling.

Forgive me my failings – in the Name of Jesus my Lord, "the same yesterday, today and for ever".   AMEN

Daily Reading

Jesus said:

"Consider the lilies of the field, how they grow; they neither toil nor spin; yet I tell you, even Solomon in all his glory was not arrayed like one of these. But if God so clothes the grass of the field, which today is alive and tomorrow is thrown into the oven, will he not much more clothe you, O men of little faith? Therefore do not be anxious, saying, 'What shall we eat?' or 'What shall we drink?' or 'What shall we wear?' For the Gentiles seek all these things; and your heavenly Father knows that you need them all. But seek first his kingdom and his righteousness, and all these things shall be yours as well."

Matthew 6:28–33

TWENTY-FOURTH DAY

In the morning

Gracious God, Creator of all good things and true, I am glad to be alive – and here.

Forgive me, wherein I have been unresponsive to Thy love and caring. I regret it now.

And I am grieved whenever I recall how often I have been critical of others for thinking and acting differently.

Many friends, up through the years, have shown me a better spirit than perhaps at times they could see in me. And I give thanks for them.

All the way, my Christian life has been a learning experience, and I give Thee thanks for that. So I am still learning.

I bless Thee for teachers, preachers, and friends who have shared a shining patience – a gift from Thyself.

I have not always loved others as they have loved me. Absorbed sometimes with my own affairs, I have "passed by".

I have not always been "the Good Samaritan" – forgive me, O God. Where there are wounds, let me offer "the sweet oils of care".

As I journey, let me never be too hurried to pause and render help. Let Christ's immortal story be alive in my daily serving.

Cruel and dispiriting experiences come to so many, I find. Use me, I pray, to translate Christ's immortal words into daily living. AMEN

In the evening

As the light dies, and night comes about all living things like a soft garment, bringing the gift of sleep, I bless Thee.

Hold in the hollow of Thy caring hand today, I pray, all just now who find life difficult and themselves sad and unsure.

Let the selfish see their actions for what they are; deliver the callous, the careless, and stir the totally unconcerned.

I remember in Thy presence some known to me in special need .... and .... and ....

Let me send each a letter, or where the distance is not great, let me pay an encouraging visit.

I commend to Thy care, this night, all my long-time needy ones, and am strengthened – as they may well be – to know that long before ever I knew and loved them, they were loved of Thee. And are still!   AMEN

Daily Reading

Paul wrote:

If I speak in the tongues of men and of angels, but have not love, I am a noisy gong or a clanging cymbal. And if I have prophetic powers, and understand all mysteries and all knowledge, and if I have all faith, so as to remove mountains, but have not love, I am nothing. If I give away all I have, and if I deliver my body to be burned, and have not love, I gain nothing.

Love is patient and kind; love is not jealous or boastful; it is not arrogant or rude. Love does not insist on its own way; it is not irritable or resentful; it does not rejoice at wrong, but rejoices in the right. Love bears all things, believes all things, endures all things.

Love never ends; as for prophecies, they will pass away; as for tongues, they will cease; as for knowledge, it will pass away.

1 Corinthians 13:1–8

TWENTY-FIFTH DAY

In the morning

Eternal God, Creator and Keeper, as the daylight comes, I waken with joy and expectation.

Thou hast kept me through the night – keep me through this day, I pray Thee.

Now I step out without fear, wholly dependent upon Thee; let me show kindness and consideration to all whom I meet.

Garrison my heart with courage, if I have to face unexpected difficulties, and bring me in at close of day, trustful as ever.

Peace and serenity are the gracious gifts I pray for now, as I mingle with many making claims on me this day.

The angers and greeds of this great world reflected in the newspapers, are never far from any of us.

Problems that confront politicians cannot be easily solved. Sustain this day everyone in a position of heavy responsibility.

Guide and direct those concerned for the Peace of the world. May nations cease from all prideful undertakings that spell war.

Only in Thy power, that upholds galaxies and fashions the seasons in their turn, can we proceed unhurt.

Only in truth and goodness and brotherhood can we survive. Teach us how to be merciful to all with whom we share life. AMEN

In the evening

Gracious Father, I am tempted to take so much for granted; forgive me, I pray.

I am tempted to fall back on words at times, without proper reverence; forgive me.

And let me rest in Thy close keeping this night; let me sleep well, and waken on the morrow refreshed.

It is a happy thought, that always countless others lie down this night with a prayer on their lips.

Watch by little children tucked in lovingly; and be especially close to little ones who are sick, or for some reason sad.

I think of .... as I lie on my pillow; and of .... who has special need this night.

I thank Thee for the peace of my home; and I remember before Thee any I know who live surrounded by family friction. AMEN

Daily Reading

He was standing by the lake of Gennesaret. And he saw two boats by the lake, but the fishermen had gone out of them and were washing their nets. Getting into one of the boats, which was Simon's, he asked him to put out a little from the land. And he sat down and taught the people from the boat. And when he had ceased speaking, he said to Simon, "Put out into the deep and let down your nets for a catch." And Simon answered, "Master, we toiled all night and took

nothing! But at your word I will let down the nets."
And when they had done this, they enclosed a great
shoal of fish.

Luke 5:1–6

TWENTY-SIXTH DAY

In the morning

O God, I ask Thy special blessing this day on all those who own the Saviourhood of Christ the world round.

May there be nothing in this day ahead of us of which we need be ashamed at the day's end;

or when we come Home at last to the close of our life's day, and behold His face.

Give us now faith to believe in the triumph of His Redeeming Love – no matter how alarming the daily news.

Give strength and glad persistence to all here who serve Him. And let us, one by one, be aware of His presence.

Bless the ongoing witness of His great Church in the world, in its ministry of forgiveness and renewal, I pray.

And grant to young people especially, the joy to be found in His service amid the affairs of life.

Enable them to add their youthfulness to the energies and prayers of all who seek for world Peace.

Let us honour faithfully the lasting values of Christ. And let our witness in our work place be to His honour and glory.

Before we set out into the busy interests of the day, let us hush our hearts, and humbly seek the guidance we need. AMEN

In the evening

At nightfall, O God, I bless Thee for this day. No two

days are ever quite the same: I bless Thee for new truths like from old settings, and for new joys.

I like to hope that today I have met strangers with a winsomeness, and readiness to help in any way I could.

Let me use as I am able, any skills with which I have been blessed; and save me from taking things too seriously.

I bless Thee for all the men and women who have enriched my life, through joys shared, books loaned, and kindly talk.

Where problems must be met, and blunders are sometimes made – forgive me, and quicken our daily relationships, I pray.

So let our comings and goings show something of the lovely spirit of Christ, in this world that stands so much in need of it. To His glory.   AMEN

Daily Reading

Jesus came to Bethany, where Lazarus was, whom Jesus had raised from the dead.

There they made him a supper; Martha served, and Lazarus was one of those at table with him.

Mary took a pound of costly ointment of pure nard and anointed the feet of Jesus and wiped his feet with her hair; and the house was filled with the fragrance of the ointment.

But Judas Iscariot, one of his disciples (he who was to betray him), said, "Why was this ointment not sold for three hundred denarii and given to the poor?"

John 12:1–5

In the morning

As I open my eyes to this new day, grant, O Lord, that I lose none of its opportunities; that I overlook none of its Christian obligations.

Let me show pleasure today in the very many gifts of life that bring no regrets in their train.

Let me not forget to be considerate of those with whom I live, and those with whom I work.

Let me be gracious to those whom I meet for the first time, and establish genuine fellowship.

Save me from the selfishness that seeks nothing but its own advantage, I pray.

Keep me persevering if the things this day holds are difficult, cheerful if anything goes wrong.

Deliver me from making excuses that in any situation I would not accept from others.

Help me this day to sustain a sweet patience with things, and with people.

So may the hours of this new day bring me to my evening's relaxation, with thankfulness;

and to my night's sleep, with Thy blessing. For Christ's sake. AMEN

In the evening

The day Thou hast given me, O God, comes to its close, and I pause a few moments to give thanks for it.

Forgive me if I have spoken any word today which now I wish had never been said;

forgive me for any action that now I wish I had never

taken. And let me show to others a like spirit of forgiveness.

I bless Thee for close, trusted friends to whom I can go at any time, without fearing myself a nuisance.

I rejoice in the good experiences we have all at some time shared, that now add up to happy memories.

I bless Thee for the satisfactions of this day's interests; and for the healthful anticipation of this night's rest.

Forgive me for tasks I began, and never finished. And let me know a joyful readiness to start again when tomorrow comes, I pray.   AMEN

Daily Reading

This is the message we have heard from him and proclaim to you, that God is light and in him is no darkness at all.

If we say we have fellowship with him while we walk in darkness, we lie and do not live according to the truth; but if we walk in the light, as he is in the light, we have fellowship with one another, and the blood of Jesus his Son cleanses us from all sin. If we say we have no sin, we deceive ourselves, and the truth is not in us. If we confess our sins, he is faithful and just, and will forgive our sins and cleanse us from all unrighteousness.

1 John 1:5–9

TWENTY-EIGHTH DAY

In the morning

O God, our Father, in Whom we live and move, and have our being –

keep us mindful today of Thy loving presence.

Let us with thankful hearts receive the gifts this day brings, and use them well.

We bless Thee for the accepted place we have in our homes, and the capacities of our minds and spirits.

We bless Thee, too, for the skills of our hands, and the opportunities to learn still more as we go.

Deliver us from envy that forgets to count our own blessings, and looks only on those of others.

For good meals to eat; and good clothes to wear; and the recurring interests of our lives, we bless Thee.

Deliver us, all the same, from a foolish content, that fails to take account of the needs of others.

Let us never fail in readiness to do for others what we can to add to their lives.

We do not wish to forget that "the Jericho Road" runs right through this way that our day knows.

We would not pass by on the other side any whom we chance on who need notice, and a helping hand.

Let us show, as we are able, the spirit of the Good Samaritan, we pray. In the Name of Christ our Lord.

AMEN

In the evening

Gracious God, our Father, bless this night those for whom the day has brought difficulties unguessed;

those who have known themselves unready for choices they discovered they had to make.

Be merciful to those who have made foolish mistakes this day for which they are sorry now.

Be supportive of those who have to admit their loneliness as night falls;

those who seem to have little capacity to reach out to others.

Deliver them from thinking only of themselves – let them begin to see how life looks to others,

and strengthen them when the new day comes, to show consideration and affection in a very real way.   AMEN

Daily Reading
Paul wrote:

I bow my knees before the Father, from whom every family in heaven and on earth is named, that according to the riches of his glory he may grant you to be strengthened with might through his Spirit . . . and that Christ may dwell in your hearts through faith; that you, being rooted and grounded in love, may have power to comprehend with all the saints what is the breadth and length and height and depth, and to know the love of Christ which surpasses knowledge, that you may be filled with all the fullness of God.

Ephesians 3:14–19

In the morning

Gracious God, I am filled with wonder at what I know
of Thee in this great world;

at each new day that follows on the rest and renewal of
night; at little new lives; at the experience of family
and friends.

Never morning light renews my awareness, but some
surprise awaits me. I bless Thee for the many-
coloured patterns of life.

I bless Thee for those who long ago planted what are
now great trees, and set roads and streets in rough
places.

I bless Thee for all who established schools, and
libraries, and rejoiced in learning.

I bless Thee for ministers and priests, nuns and
deaconesses, for Christian scholars, and all deeply
aware of spiritual values.

Today, they are many more in number – with young men
and women humbly coming forward to join their
ranks.

I bless Thee, too, for all parents, who joyously, naturally
share within their homes the glories of the Gospel.

And for all missionaries who have answered Thy call
into far places and unknown situations, I bless Thee.

Let me this day, where life finds me, be a faithful
follower of the Living Christ, an interpreter of His
Spirit.   AMEN

O Lord, have mercy upon all who have brought suffering upon themselves, or others this day;

on all who have grown cynical, and forgetful of the goodness of life; on any who thoughtlessly have not raised grateful hearts to pray.

Bless and sustain those battling alone with problems, and bring them, of their own choice, to an acceptance of Thy help.

Hold in Thy special care this day any who suffer injustice; any who find their secret store of courage sinking low.

Sustain the lonely and the shy, and those who have no experience of supportive fellowship with others about them.

We are all insufficient in ourselves. We need Thy divine support – not only daily, but especially when we come to the crossroads of choice.

Let us lean for our sufficiency upon the Gospel of Thy grace; and go upon our way, praising Thy Son, our Saviour.   AMEN

Daily Reading

Paul wrote to his Christian friends:

Do you not know that in a race all the runners compete, but only one receives the prize? So run that you may obtain it. Every athlete exercises self-control in all things. They do it to receive a perishable wreath, but we an imperishable. Well, I do not run aimlessly, I do not box as one beating the air; but I pommel my body and subdue it, lest after preaching to others I myself should be disqualified.

1 Corinthians 9:24–27

THIRTIETH DAY

In the morning

Gracious God, may my heart be ready to welcome in this new day. I delight in my new energies. Let me use them wisely.

May no past sin of stupidity stand in the way of my service. Forgive me that ever I have moved casually through Thy great world;

that ever I have borne witness, thoughtless of lives quickened. Let me be constantly on the tip-toe of expectancy.

Thou art the Creator of surprises and miracles all about me. Every Spring reminds me of this recurring wonder.

But more than this, I rejoice in the renewal of Thy forgiveness, and for new beauties revealed in human character.

Lord of the Empty Tomb, and the Stone rolled away, I would join eagerly with those who first ran with the Good News.

Bless this day all missionaries, Christian teachers, authors, speakers and translators who as eagerly share the Easter Gospel.

My heart dances this day in the reality of this greatest Miracle. Let me continue to put my trust in the Living Christ.

Bless my voice, quicken my every faculty, and lead me ever into fuller discipleship, I pray.

For the sweet fellowship of kindred spirits, I never cease to praise Thy holy Name. AMEN

In the evening

As I look back over my chosen field of work here, I ask Thee to strip from it anything unworthy.

Thou knowest my longing to add to the rich sum total of life. Thou hast lent me skills, and warmed my heart's affections.

Grant that I may have an offering of worth at the day's end. I bless Thee for my family, my friends, and neighbours true;

for all whose record of fine living has reached me through books; for the challenge to join here in service of Thy Kingdom;

for the many who, for Thy sake, assume great responsibilities; for those who move into government and administration, I seek Thine aid.

Reveal Thyself anew to those who must walk a solitary way. Sustain all who are set on the making of Peace among us.

Let our national grievances be done away with, and a new age dawn. In the lasting power of Jesus Christ, Thy Son, our Lord. AMEN

Daily Reading

Jesus said:

"In praying do not heap up empty phrases . . . Pray then like this:

'Our Father who art in heaven,
Hallowed be thy name.
Thy kingdom come,

Thy will be done,
   On earth as it is in heaven.
Give us this day our daily bread;
And forgive us our debts,
   As we also have forgiven our
      debtors;
And lead us not into temptation,
   But deliver us from evil.'

For if you forgive men their trespasses, your heavenly
Father also will forgive you; but if you do not forgive
men their trespasses, neither will your Father forgive
your trespasses."

Matthew 6:7,9–15

In the morning

O God, our Father, every day comes from Thee filled with new opportunities, and we believe this will be the same.

Keep our eyes wide open to things of beauty and lasting significance today.

Let me continue to count people more important than things, and Love that issues in service the most important of all.

We bless Thee for the living example of Jesus, and the stirring record of His life set down in the New Testament.

We rejoice in good men and women who have loved and served Him truly, since He called His first disciples.

And let us do that, here and now, in this modern century – full of wonderful opportunities as well as of tangled problems.

Strengthen our hearts, we pray, by the constant reminder of Thine unchanged Love.

Save us from falling to the same faults, and the same temptations, time and time again. Let us make of life a spontaneous offering to Thee.

We have no power in ourselves to do this in our earth-life; but Thou art our Eternal Father, for ever, Whose greatest Gift to us is Jesus Christ, Thy beloved Son.

AMEN

In the evening

In all our comings and our goings through the years, Thy

Love and Guidance is unquestioned; and we go on.
Thou hast never left us to travel this way alone, and we
    are lastingly glad of that.
We have so little wisdom of our own, so little vision; so
    little strength of body and spirit.
But with Thy wonderful Love embracing us always, Thy
    lasting forgiveness when again and again we fail, we
    are not afraid of this life here, or of the life to come.

AMEN

Daily Reading

Now the eleven disciples went to Galilee, to the mountain to which Jesus had directed them. And when they saw him they worshipped him; but some doubted.

And Jesus came and said to them, "All authority in heaven and on earth has been given to me. Go therefore and make disciples of all nations, baptizing them in the name of the Father and of the Son and of the Holy Spirit, teaching them to observe all that I have commanded you; and lo, I am with you always, to the close of the age."

Matthew 28:16–20

PART TWO

Affirmations for Sleepless Hours

Let nothing disturb thee;
Let nothing dismay thee;
All things pass:
God never changes.

Saint Teresa

Speak to Him for He hears, and Spirit with spirit can meet –
Closer is He than breathing, and nearer than hands and feet.

Tennyson

It does not matter that I cannot hold on to God – He holds on to me.

R.F.S

Deep peace of the Running Wave to you,
Deep peace of the Flowing Air to you,
Deep peace of the Quiet Earth to you,
Deep peace of the Shining Stars to you,
Deep peace of the Son of Peace to you.

A Celtic Benediction

Christ is a Person to be trusted.

Dr Ronald Selby Wright

Who shall separate us from the love of Christ? shall tribulation, or distress, or persecution, or famine, or nakedness, or peril, or sword? . . .

Nay, in all these things we are more than conquerors through him that loved us.

For I am persuaded that neither death, nor life, nor angels, nor principalities, nor powers, nor things present, nor things to come, nor height, nor depth, nor any other creature, shall be able to separate us from the love of God, which is in Christ Jesus our Lord.

Saint Paul (Romans 8:35,37–39; Authorized Version)

He is not a God of the dead, but of the living: for all live unto Him.

Dr Luke (Luke 20:38)

Thou hast destined us for change, us and all things Thy hands have made . . .

We fear not. Nay, rather, we are jubilant. Hast Thou not loved us before the world began? What can change bring us – but some better thing?

Alistair Maclean (from *Hebridean Altars*)

Our solace in suffering is that the Man of Sorrows is sure to pass this way.

Helen Keller

Not by appointment does one meet Sorrow;
it comes out of the complexities of human
belonging –
swift with dark foreboding – making poorer,
or richer. Who can say?
Holding unnoticed silences apart,
unnoticed contentments,
it breaks the floodgates

of one's whole being.
Easy words slip from one's shoulders
like a slight shawl;
only Faith in God that goes deep,
goes deep enough;
for He has suffered, too,
and alone knows how to heal,
to sift from grief
eternal victory,
eternal gain.

R.F.S.

There is nothing love cannot face; there is no limit to its faith, its hope, and its endurance.

Saint Paul (1 Corinthians 13:7; New English Bible)

What though my joys and comforts die,
The Lord, my Saviour liveth!
What though the darkness gather round,
Songs in the night He giveth!

"Praise", by Robert Lowry

Prayer does not always banish my difficulty – but it brings it to the place where I am sharing it with Christ.

R.F.S

There is no Sorrow, Lord, too light
To bring in prayer to Thee;
Nor is there any care too slight
To wake Thy sympathy.

Thou Who hast trod the thorny road
  Wilt share each small distress;
The love which bore the greater load
  Will not refuse the less.

Hymn by Jane Crewdson

"God . . . giveth us richly all things to enjoy", said St Paul to young Timothy in the first Christian century. And things were not easy then (1 Timothy 6:17; A.V.). But this is a shining truth. I have heard it misread as "all things to *endure*" by someone having trouble with the light, or with his spectacles – or was it with his Faith?

R.F.S

Let not Thy Love grow dim, dear God,
  Nor sense of Thee depart.
Let not the memory of Thy word
  Burn low within my heart.

Anon.

We are not here to be beaten. We are here, the weakest of us, to be "more than conquerors". A deep Faith in the sovereignty of God overthrows the tyranny of things.

Dr George Morrison

Ordinary people, if they want religion at all, want it to live by, not merely to think about.

Dr Russell Maltby

The dawn is not distant,
Nor is the night starless;
  Love is Eternal!
God is still God, and
  His Faith shall not fail us,
Christ is Eternal!

Anon.

O Lord our God, Thy children need Thee yet,
  Their feet to guide, their hearts with Love to fill;
O give the quicken'd ear, lest we forget
  That Thou art speaking still.

R. Walmsley

Each day we may see some new thing in Christ. *His Love* hath neither brim nor bottom.

Samuel Rutherford

Here then is the gist of Christianity for you in a single sentence: At the centre of the Universe there is that which is *more like a father's loving heart than like anything else we know*.

Dr John Baillie

Quiet now . . .
Close the mind's door
On business of the day
And for this brief moment
Clear the way
For God.

Helen F. Couch

You need not cry out very loud; He is nearer than you think.

> Brother Lawrence (seventeenth century
> – and still wonderfully true)

Thou takest the pen – and the lines dance,
Thou takest the flute – and the notes shimmer,
Thou takest the brush – and the colours sing,
So all things have meaning and beauty . . .
Where Thou art.
How then can I hold back anything from Thee?

> The late Dag Hammarskjöld (1905–62),
> United Nations Secretary-General

May I be no man's enemy, but friend of that which
   abides;
May I never quarrel with those nearest me: and if I do,
May I be reconciled quickly.

> Eusebius (third century)

Lord of all power and might, Who art the Author and
Giver of all good things; graft in our hearts the love
of Thy Name; increase in us true religion; nourish us
with all goodness, and of Thy great mercy keep us in
the same; through Jesus Christ our Lord.   AMEN

> Book of Common Prayer

The Eternal God is my Refuge, and underneath are the
everlasting arms.

> Deuteronomy 33:27

Now thank we all our God,
    With heart and hands and voices,
Who wondrous things hath done,
    In Whom His world rejoices;
Who from our mothers' arms,
    Hath blessed us on our way,
With countless gifts of love,
    And still is ours today.
                A hymn of praise from Martin Rinkart

PART THREE

Psalms for Sunday Mornings

FIRST SUNDAY

Create in me a clean heart, O God,
    and put a new and right spirit
        within me.
Cast me not away from thy presence,
    and take not thy holy Spirit
        from me.

Psalm 51:10–11

SECOND SUNDAY

O come, let us worship and bow down,
    let us kneel before the Lord,
        our Maker!
For he is our God,
    and we are the people of his
        pasture,
    and the sheep of his hand.

Psalm 95:6–7

THIRD SUNDAY

Make a joyful noise to the Lord, all
        the earth;
    break forth into joyous song and sing
        praises!
Sing praises to the Lord with the lyre,
    with the lyre and the sound of melody!

Psalm 98:4–5

FOURTH SUNDAY

Make a joyful noise to the Lord,
    all the lands!
Serve the Lord with gladness!
Come into his presence with singing!
Know that the Lord is God!
It is he that made us, and we are his.

                              Psalm 100:1–3

FIFTH SUNDAY

Unless the Lord builds the house,
    those who build it labour in vain.
Unless the Lord watches over the city,
    the watchman stays awake in vain.
It is in vain that you rise up early
        and go late to rest,
eating the bread of anxious toil;
    for he gives to his beloved sleep.

                              Psalm 127:1–2

PART FOUR

Prayers for Special Days

A TIME OUT WITH NATURE

Great Creator, I praise Thee for the beauty I find out of
　doors;
　　　for new life that rises from tiny seeds;
　　　for flowers rejoicing in many colours;
　　　and trees towering high with strength and shade.
I praise Thee, too, for fragrances hidden in secret
　places;
　　　for shapes that surprise me again and again;
　　　for fine twigs filigreed against the sky;
　　　for birds that greet the day with song.
I praise Thee for mountains and hills up-rising;
　　　for plains and valleys spread afar;
　　　and rivers and streams making towards the sea.
　　　I marvel at the diversity of Thy Creation –
So rich it is in opportunity for work and leisure.　　AMEN

A PRAYER FOR ONE LIVING ALONE

Gracious Lord, I am one of very many now living alone;
　　　yet truly, I am not alone, for Thou art with me;
　　　and I have dear friends in and out – as I can manage.
　　　Within and without, I have much to do.
But this home that once I shared is still dear to me;
　　　our things are all about me, and I care for them
　　　since Death led my dear one gently on her way.
　　　Some now live alone of long-time choice;
some because of marriage estrangement lastingly
　painful;

111

others, at the end of the family, with inherited property.

Give us each courage, and gentleness of spirit,
and keep us still strong in Faith, I pray,

until, at the end of this earth-life, we come to our Eternal Home. AMEN

BEFORE I OPEN MY BIBLE

O Lord of Light and Truth, Thou hast enriched my life with books – my shelves are full.

Old and new they are – the latest with bright jackets.

But the most cherished is the Bible that I read at this hour.

Unlike any other book, it cannot be read straight through.

But I remember always that it is a progressive revelation, for all that it is not a book of a scientific age.

I find beauty in the many types of literature it uses – poetry, history, story, song, letter and gospel.

I pray for an alert and reverent mind as I turn its pages, and a continued readiness to embrace the Truth there awaiting me.

I know myself especially blessed – since in the early days of our race, men and women lacked this priceless revelation.

Bless this day, I pray, scholars, teachers, translators, and all who serve the Bible Societies world-wide, for Christ's sake. AMEN

AS I SET OUT SHOPPING

Eternal Father, my commonplace needs are known to
  Thee;

but occasionally I am tempted.

Give me good judgement today, I pray,

and save me from every kind of extravagance.

All Nature about me, blessed by Thee, is beautifully
  clothed –

hills, beasts and birds, and domestic pets.

I thank Thee for their simple companionship; enable me
  to be faithful whilst they are in my care.

And let me be as suitably clothed, I pray –

and pleasing, though seeking no flattery. Indoors and
  out, let me add some attraction to Thy creation.

AMEN

AS I GO WITH OTHERS TO CHURCH

O God, Holy and Great, Whose word is in the frame-
work of the world; shining in the spirit of man in his high
moments, reveal Thyself anew to us this day. Let Thy
glorious revelation through Jesus Christ – made Man to
greet us on this earth, with Redeeming Love – be very
real.

It is wonderful to realize ourselves – many or few –
part of Thine immense Church on earth. Use our
fellowship to stimulate the discipleship of others, and let
Thy Spirit be felt in all our comings and goings. We
would not cherish creeds more than the living witness of
Thy Kingdom. We would not limit our religion to pews

113

and pulpits. Wherever life finds us, there enable us to witness to Christ, our Risen Lord and Saviour. So may His power and grace reach needy men and women everywhere.

AMEN

FINDING MYSELF IN HOSPITAL

God, infinite in Love and Mercy, I need to know Thee near in this hour. Support all who bear responsibility in this busy place, and also my relations and friends when they go home to talk over things.

I pray especially for doctors and nurses, for office staff and for ambulance men; and for all who serve behind the scenes. For those whose service is centred in the laboratory; for those largely taken for granted – porters and ward-maids; for those who cook meals, or who serve them temptingly. I pray also for those who tend the coming and going of mail; those dealing with flowers, or pushing the library trolleys through the wards; and those delivering the daily newspapers.

For every kind of supportive service, I give Thee thanks, O God. I pray especially for the chaplains, finding their way helpfully in and out of the wards. Comfort all those unsure of procedures; all facing operations; all feeling lonely; all finding their recovery long, and waiting to go home. Sustain their patience and hope, I pray Thee, in the Name of the Great Physician.

AMEN

SETTING OFF ON HOLIDAY

O God, Source of all good and Guide of all my days, it is lovely to have leisure – to be rising later in the mornings; to be having unusual meals; and to be mixing with little-known people. I do not forget that whilst I relax, others must work. Let me show courtesy to all who serve me.

Let me keep my eyes open for things of interest and beauty. In the immensity of the sky, mountains raised up, and the fertility of grass and gardens, I find joy. In the sight and song of birds, and the delight of furry creatures; in crickets and grasshoppers, and gauzy wings of dragonflies; in the varied tints and graceful shapes of leaves; in seasonal flowers in their gay colours; in trees offering shade, and the refreshment of breezes – I rejoice. I offer thanks for streams, for rivers and lakes, and quiet seasides, for the unceasing play and pull of the tides. For all those who for a time share these things with me, I give thanks.

Let me still find my way to church on Sundays; and in Thy mercy, keep safely, I pray, all those I love at home.

AMEN

GIVING THANKS FOR GOOD BOOKS AND MAGAZINES

O God, truth and delight come to me in so many ways.
  I bless Thee for the capacity to read.
Let me choose well; and accept my thanks for fine
  authors, publishers and booksellers. Especially
  accept my thanks for reading friends and associates,
  ready to lend books and magazines.

Bless all librarians, I pray, and deliver them from the ruts of routine. Bless especially all who take delight in teaching little children to read.

So may beauty and goodness and joy be spread abroad. For Thy Name's sake. AMEN

MY BIRTHDAY

O God, this is a day that seems to come round so soon. I offer Thee my thanks for mercies throughout the year.

Thou hast granted me physical strength enough for my needs; and joys of mind and spirit.

I have seen Thy greatness and goodness revealed in Nature – each changing season, with its shapes and colours.

I bless Thee for family life; for little new lives that have joined us on our way. We thank Thee for their innocence and trust.

We bless Thee for friends who for years have come over our doorstep, for experiences shared, and outings together.

Some things I have done that would have been better undone. Forgive me. And for things talked of, that could have been left unsaid.

Go with me, I pray, from this birthday on into the unknown year now opening before me.

And keep me in my goings-out, and my comings-in, now and always, for Christ's sake. AMEN

O God of glad hearts, I am only one of many in this place who this day rejoice that long ago Jesus began His ministry as Guest at a modest wedding of two young people, in Cana of Galilee. May we be as happily aware of His presence here today.

We are glad that the New Testament account of that day made room to tell us that His Mother Mary also was there; along with His disciple friends (John 2:1–2).

Thou art our God of enduring Love and good judgement, Who "setteth the solitary in families" – as the Psalmist rejoiced to tell us (Psalm 68:6; A.V.). We give thanks in this hour that it is still Thy plan to call a man and a woman to preside over the building of a home, into which little new lives may be born, and where steady relations and friends may come.

Let the years bring from Thine undiminished sources of Love, to these two who stand here in Thy Holy Presence, the blessings Thou art so ready to give.

If they, at any time, are required together to climb hard places and high, give them gentle, loving patience, and courage. May the light of Thy Spirit, which has served so many, illume their hearts and direct their paths. We ask this in the Name of Jesus, the Chief Guest still.   AMEN

Morning

God, guide our hearts this happy day to the very centre of this celebration.

Once, long ago, Wise Men from the East learnt the language of a Star set to guide them.

They made Time's Greatest Discovery. Then and there, bending low, they presented royal gifts.

Since then their secret has belonged to all mankind, and so has come to us. We do our best to remember that joyously this day.

Bless all children sharing the Festival with us – let us not miss out the retelling of the story.

Little ones everywhere excitedly welcome their giving and receiving. But let our celebration be centred gladly on *One Child*.

Bless too, we beseech Thee, all parents and relations busy making meals, and welcoming guests.

Sweeten all moods today; keep us mindful of the lonely, the poor, the hungry.

As we sing our carols and delight in our decorations, remind us of any near at hand with empty stockings.

Bless everyone gathered in church – this whole world round – to sing Christ's praises, just now. Let us continue to receive His love into our lives.   AMEN

Evening

Father, this has been a day to remember gladly; and we praise Thee for it.

There has been all day no "generation gap" – old and young alike have had their part in this glad Festival.

Gifts, good food and fun have had their place. And now at last night has come; and the little ones make towards bed.

The old and the frail remember the keeping of one more Christmas, to add to their rich recollections.

Bless this bedtime all who, in hospitals and institutions, have today shared in story-telling, or spent time cooking, singing or entertaining.

And let none of us forget that first must come "Glory to God", before ever we can have "Peace on earth".

AMEN

NEW YEAR'S DAY

Morning

Gracious God, I can never bypass the wonder of beginning again, and I give thanks for this special day.

As I look back over the old year, there are a few things I would like to forget. As I name them, grant me Thy forgiveness.

But as I take time to look back, I am aware of many mercies. Today, I would bring them to the front of my mind.

I bless Thee for companionship of those I love; I rejoice in good talk, in shared interests, and homes in cities and towns.

I recall gardens and trees and wide spaces in Nature; I

remember rivers and lakes, great beaches and
waterfalls;

I give thanks for all preachers, authors and friends who
have strengthened my Faith this year past.

I rejoice in my association with Thy Church in this part
of the world. I remember all who worship with me.

As young men and women become aware of a call to
minister, guide them as they set about their studies.

Support this year all who have grown old in Thy service;
all who cannot now read as widely as once they did,
or travel as far.

Give us all the unvarying assurance of Thy Love and
keeping, evermore. In the Name of Christ, our Lord.

AMEN

The Year's First Evening

Already, My Father, possibilities of a new beginning are
with me. I can see some areas where this could make
a great difference.

Forgiven and renewed, I am ready to go on – despite
past failures – for Thy loving support is unending.

In all sincerity, enable me to serve. Let me interpret
Love through body, mind and spirit.

Let me rejoice in steady obedience. Lead me eagerly
into further Truth, that as the days pass, I may be
enriched in personality.

Let the accumulated experience of mounting years add
to my usefulness, here and now.

I give Thee thanks for more books and music and art
added this year; and so many new beautiful things.

I rejoice in all known to me who are newly come into the
service of Thy Kingdom, O Lord. Give me a share in
helping them, I pray. AMEN

GOOD FRIDAY

Morning
I find it difficult, O God, to summon up words for this
day of Crucifixion. The Gospels are so imprinted on
my mind.
I can only think that I will be relieved and thankful when
the day is through.
But it holds something precious at the very heart of my
Faith. I try to link myself with that little group around
the Cross.
I bless Thee, O God, for the faithful women especially.
Though it holds a grim solitariness in sacrifice,
and it bespeaks a measure of forgiveness I cannot
imagine, yet it extends the arms of the Cross, to reach
the ends of the whole world.
I marvel at the care of Christ for the two suffering
alongside Him; I am sincerely, deeply moved by His
care for His Mother.
And it seems wonderful that He there laid a task on
friend John – looking into the days to come.
I bless Thee for the generosity of Joseph of Arimathea
in offering his own new tomb, that Jesus might know
some dignity in Death.

Against such, the dastardly deeds of those within the Judgement Hall stand out so cruelly. Imagination falls short!

We see but a glint of Roman armour, and the night's flickering torches – but the range and depth of the whole happening is far beyond our human comprehension.   AMEN

Evening

O God, I can hardly wait to have this sad day pass – on its way to a third day holding resurrection and triumph!

Help me, in humility, to use this day well, placed for all Time in the calendar of Thy World Church.

As we read the Gospels this day, let them issue in us a finer discipleship; so may we sing our solemn hymns, and prepare our hearts for Easter Day.

So may we each, in deepest sincerity, borrow Thomas's words, as he reached out his hand to know his Master truly risen –

and found himself moved to exclaim: "*My Lord, and my God!*"   AMEN

EASTER DAY

Morning

O Lord of Life, my heart is full of joy this day as I recount the story of the world's First Easter.

I bless Thee for those who came early to Christ's Tomb with sweet spices, a sign of their love. I rejoice in their loyalty.

What a wonderful lifting of grief it was, to find the Stone rolled away! And to be supported by other faithful hearts!

Most of all, I bless Thee for Mary's meeting with the Master, risen from the dead, and speaking her name!

I bless Thee for this greatest News, that came out of the Garden that Easter morn.

I rejoice in the faith of those who soon carried the News far and wide. Enable me today to put away all thought of defeat.

Quicken my loyalty and love with a lasting certainty of triumph! I bless Thee for the experience of the Emmaus Road.

To any of us cast down, let there come the same living Presence, and with the lifting of bowed heads, the speeding of tired feet to tell others.

Again and again, as one by one we have sung "Abide with me!", Thou hast renewed this in our day.

So may we all continue on our way, supported by this reality, deeply, sincerely experienced.   AMEN

Evening

Gracious God, draw near with compassion to all who know grief, lagging time, and a dark future;

give them of the experience of the first followers of Jesus, with their hearts overcoming the grimness of Death.

We take courage from their courage, who as the new dawn came, arose and went forward to Life!

We give thanks for their glorious transformation. And for the triumph in which now we too have a part!

Never now shall we be cast down by Despair, nor by
Death. At the heart of our Faith is a Garden – with
its Open Tomb!

Keep us faithful in the proclamation of this News, we
pray, and speed our feet to the ends of the earth!

Let us live as assuredly as we hope to, this day and ever!
So will Easter, for us, never end!   AMEN

WHITSUNDAY

Morning

At this day's beginning, O God, I make an effort to
visualize the obedient company that awaited the
coming of Christ's Spirit.

They were, for the most part, ordinary people; but it was
a dramatic happening – and has never been forgotten.

Year by year, the world Church holds it in memory, and
many times in between reads the New Testament
account of it.

It is Thy holy lasting gift to replace fearfulness with
Faith; dullness with vitality; self-absorption with
unselfish love.

It banishes from Christ's disciples self-superiority,
disloyalty and carelessness.

It empowers men and women to witness compellingly to
Thy love, to present the winsomeness of the ongoing
Gospel in the earth.

I bless Thee for all who treasure this gift today; all who
remember with humble thankfulness the first coming
of His Spirit.

O God, the world about me is very captivating – give me a stronger link with my Risen, Ascended Lord.

And withal, give me a winsome humility in all this day's undertakings, as I go about my ordinary affairs.

Bless my allegiance – and let me walk closely with my fellow disciples of Christ here and now, I pray.   AMEN

Evening

O God, as I lie down to sleep at day's end, I am moved to joy at the lasting significance of this day.

I cannot think of the world without the first Pentecost; nor the work of the Church through the centuries, without its witness.

Let us show an overall Christian concern for the Kingdom – of which Jesus spoke continually when He was here among men and women.

Let our modern-day care for our fellows rejoice His heart – and may we show His courage for the problems that must be met.

I myself do not deserve all Thy mercies, but Thy love is unending, Thy power beyond all appearances, energizing simple people.

At Pentecost those gathered shared great things, and many went forth into the world persons remade. For this, we praise Thee.   AMEN

ALL SAINTS' DAY

O God, I am glad that this day – the first of November – is still called "All Saints' Day" in our modern world. It passes for many, we know, without so much as a thought.

125

But we praise Thee on this day for the very many men and women who up through the centuries have glorified Thee. Many – in earlier times, it is true – suffered persecution and death, at the hands of the ignorant and merciless.

We bless Thee for their courage, not forgetting the many in camps and prisons the world round, for this same Faith today.

Most have been "saints without haloes", and we have been privileged to know a goodly number.

We bless Thee for their unquestioning love, their steadfastness and self-forgetfulness – their Christ-like-ness – not just in their words, but in their lives.

Enable us, in turn, one by one, to follow their lead, in the Service of Christ.   AMEN

*

(*Note*)

Before we accept the reality of a New Testament phrase, "Called to be saints", which was coined for groups of Christians in many ways like ourselves, we need to understand from New Testament scholars that saints were not *perfect* people. The New Testament word for a thing or person spotlessly clean was *hieros*; but the word *hagios*, translated "saint", has always been anything or any person – whatever its nature, past history, or use – *now wholly offered to God*. And we are encouraged – for not even Saint Peter and Saint Paul were perfect people; and there were "Saints in Caesar's household". "To be a saint", as a modern scholar has put it for us, "is to know God as the Great Reality, to belong to Him in supreme devotion; and to live in daily service to one's fellows, for His sake."

*

Let our last thought shared in this book
  be from the poet George MacDonald:
"God only knows how happy He could make us,
  if only we would let Him!"